Religions of the World
Sikhism

Sue Penney

Heinemann
LIBRARY

www.heinemann.co.uk/library

Visit our website to find out more information about Heinemann Library books.

To order:
 Phone 44 (0) 1865 888066
 Send a fax to 44 (0) 1865 314091
Visit the Heinemann Bookshop at www.heinemann.co.uk/library to browse our catalogue and order online.

First published in Great Britain by Heinemann Library
Halley Court, Jordan Hill, Oxford OX2 8EJ
a division of Reed Educational & Professional Publishing Ltd.
Heinemann is a registered trademark of Reed Educational & Professional Publishing Ltd.

OXFORD MELBOURNE AUCKLAND JOHANNESBURG BLANTYRE GABORONE
IBADAN PORTSMOUTH NH (USA) CHICAGO

Designed by Ken Vail Graphic Design, Cambridge
Originated by Universal
Printed by Wing King Tong in Hong Kong.

ISBN 0 431 14951 8
06 05 04 03 02
10 9 8 7 6 5 4 3 2 1

British Library Cataloguing in Publication Data

Penney, Sue
Sikhism. – (Religions of the world)
1. Sikhism – Juvenile literature
I. Title
294.6

Acknowledgements
The Publishers would like to thank the following for permission to reproduce photographs:
Ann and Bury Peerless pp. 11, 21, 27, 28, 33; Circa Photo Library pp. 9, 10, 32, 35, 42; Harjinder Singh Sagoo pp. 4, 8, 14, 15, 16, 19, 22, 24, 25, 26, 29, 31, 34, 36, 38, 39, 40, 41, 43; Hutchison p. 37; Impact p. 30; Judy Harrison/Format p. 20; Phil and Val Emmett pp. 6, 12, 17, 18, 24.

Cover photograph reproduced with permission of Circa Photo Library.

Our thanks to Philip Emmett for his comments in the preparation of this book.

Every effort has been made to contact copyright holders of any material reproduced in this book. Any omissions will be rectified in subsequent printings if notice is given to the Publisher.

Words appearing in the text in bold, **like this**, are explained in the Glossary.

Contents

Dates: in this book, dates are followed by the letters BCE (Before Common Era) or CE (Common Era). This is instead of using BC (Before Christ) and AD (*Anno Domini*, meaning In the year of our Lord), which is a Christian system. The date numbers are the same in both systems.

Introducing Sikhism

Sikhs meet for worship in a gurdwara.

Sikhs are followers of the religion called Sikhism. Sikhism began about 500 years ago in the part of India called the Punjab. Today there are Sikhs in many countries of the world. The word Sikh comes from the **Punjabi** language which many Sikhs speak. It means 'someone who learns' – in other words someone who is a pupil or a follower.

Gurus

Sikhs follow the teachings of **Gurus**. In India, the word guru is a title which is often given to teachers of religion. Sikhs believe that there were ten Gurus who were very special. They believe that these Gurus came to the world to give God's teachings to human beings. Sikhs believe these teachings show them how to live.

Facts about Sikhism

- *Sikhism began in India in the fifteenth century CE. It was started by Guru Nanak.*
- *Sikhs believe that Guru Nanak was the first of ten Gurus who were especially important.*
- *The Sikh holy book is called the Guru Granth Sahib.*
- *The Sikh place of worship is called a **gurdwara**, which means Guru's door.*
- *There are about 20 million Sikhs in the world today.*

The first Guru of the Sikhs was called Guru Nanak. The tenth Guru said that there would be no more living Gurus. Instead, the Guru would be the Sikhs' holy book, which is called the **Guru Granth Sahib**.

What do Sikhs believe?

Sikhs believe in one God who is almighty and **eternal**. Sikhs believe that God made the universe and everything in it, and that God is present everywhere and in everything. God is good and cares about everything, too. Sikhs believe that God is a **spirit** who should be loved and worshipped.

▲ *The Sikh symbol is called a khanda. It is a symbol of the power of God.*

Sikhs believe that God created male and female, but that God is a spirit who is neither male nor female. Because of this, Sikhs take care never to describe God as being male or female. This is why they never say 'he' or 'she' when talking about God.

The Sikh symbol

The Sikh **symbol** is called a **khanda**. Two swords on the outside show that Sikhs should fight for what is right. Between them is a circle, which shows that God is one, and has no beginning or end. In the centre is a two-edged sword, also called a khanda, showing the power of God.

The Sikh Gurus – Guru Nanak

Pictures of Guru Nanak often show him looking like this.

Guru Nanak was the first **Guru** of the Sikhs. He was born in 1469 CE in a village called Talwandi in northern India. Today this place is in Pakistan and is called Nankana Sahib. It was given this name to remember Guru Nanak.

In India in the fifteenth century CE, most people followed one of two religions. They were either **Hindus** or **Muslims**. Nanak was brought up to be a Hindu. When he grew up, he worked with people who were Muslims. Nanak enjoyed talking to people about what they believed, and he learned a lot about both these religions. Nanak married when he was 19 years old, and he and his wife had two sons.

Nanak's vision

One morning when he was about 30 years old, Nanak went to bathe in the river as usual. Then he disappeared. Everyone thought he had drowned. When he returned, he did not speak for a whole day. Then he said that while he was away he had had a **vision**. He said that he had been shown that it is not important which religion people follow. What really matters is the way people live. Nanak said that God had told him to spend the rest of his life teaching people. In India, a respected teacher of religion is called a guru. Nanak became known as Guru Nanak, but he called himself Nanak Das, which means God's servant.

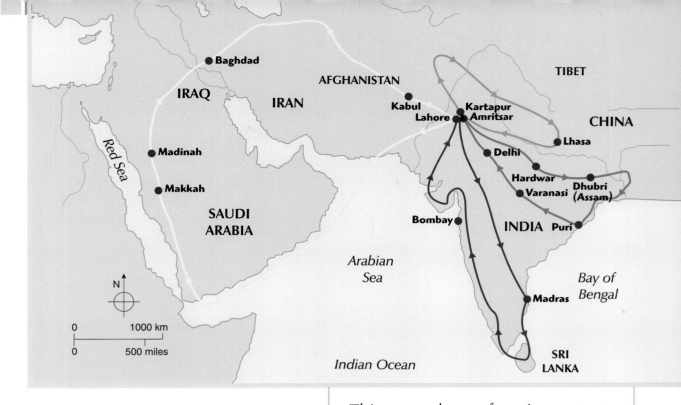

The first Sikhs

▲ *This map shows four important journeys that Guru Nanak made.*

Guru Nanak travelled from place to place, teaching people, for many years. Eventually, he settled in a village called Kartapur in northern India. A group of people who wanted to follow Guru Nanak's teachings came to live nearby. They became the first Sikhs. The followers often ate together, and this became an important part of their life in Kartapur. In India at that time people from different **castes** never ate together.

Just before he passed away (Sikhs often avoid saying that the Gurus died) in 1534 CE, Guru Nanak chose a follower called Lehna to be the next Guru. He gave him a new name, Angad, which means 'part of me'.

Guru Nanak's journeys

Guru Nanak spent twenty years of his life travelling. He went to Varanasi, the holy city for Hindus. He went to Makkah, the holy city for Muslims, and he went to many other places, too. Everywhere he went, he taught people that what matters is the way a person lives.

The Sikh Gurus (2)

After **Guru** Nanak, there were nine other Gurus. Each one was chosen by the one before, and they each continued Guru Nanak's teachings. They all worked in different ways to develop the new religion of Sikhism. The dates after their names here show when they were Guru.

Guru Angad (1539–52 CE)

You can find the places mentioned in this book on the map on page 44.

Guru Angad, the second Guru, was chosen by Guru Nanak himself. Guru Angad began providing education for young people. He developed the **Gurmukhi** alphabet in which the Sikh holy books are written. Gurmukhi is the written form of the **Punjabi** language. Until then, Punjabi was a spoken language, not a written one. Guru Angad wanted to be able to write down Guru Nanak's **hymns**. Guru Angad also began building **gurdwaras**, where Sikhs worship. Before Guru Angad passed away at the age of 48, he chose Amar Das to be the next Guru.

Guru Amar Das (1552–74 CE)

Guru Amar Das was 73 years old when he became the third Guru. He began building a new city at Amritsar, in the Punjab in India. This became the holiest place for Sikhs.

*The **Guru Granth Sahib** is written in Gurmukhi. This way of writing was invented by Guru Angad.*

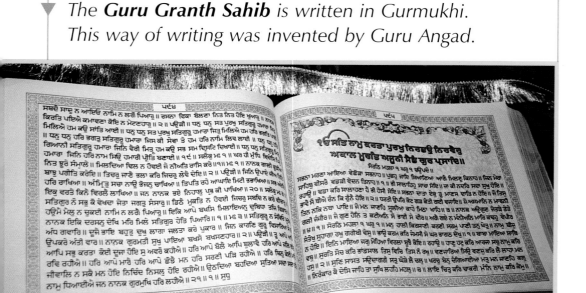

Guru Amar Das encouraged Sikhs to meet three times a year at festival times. They came to Goindwal, where he lived. This meant that the Guru could meet all Sikhs, and everyone could listen to the Guru's teaching. Like Guru Nanak, Guru Amar Das also encouraged everyone to eat together. This is a very important part of Sikhism, and it still continues today. The meal is called the **langar**, and it is so important that the room in the gurdwara where the meal is eaten has the same name.

Before he passed away at the age of 95, Guru Amar Das chose his son-in-law, Jetha, to be the next Guru.

Guru Ram Das (1574–81 CE)

When he became Guru, Jetha chose to change his name. He was called Guru Ram Das, which means 'servant of God'. He continued building the city of Amritsar, which Guru Amar Das had begun. It became a great city for trade and the most important city for the Sikh religion. Guru Ram Das is remembered especially for writing the **Lavan**, the hymn which is always used at Sikh weddings.

▲ The langar has always been an important part of Sikhism.

The ten Gurus

Sikhs often say that the Gurus were like lamps that have been lit from one another. They each worked for the good of people and of Sikhism.

The Sikh Gurus (3)

Guru Arjan (1581–1606 CE)

Guru Arjan was the son of Guru Ram Das. He began building the **Harimandir Sahib**, the Golden Temple in Amritsar in India. Guru Arjan also collected together **hymns** by Sikh Gurus and other writers. He made them into the Sikhs' first holy book, called the **Adi Granth**. Later, the Adi Granth would be called the **Guru Granth Sahib**. Guru Arjan was killed because he refused to give up his Sikh faith, even though the ruler of the country had said that he must.

Baba Buddha

*Baba Buddha lived from 1506–1631. He was a great Sikh. He knew all the first six Gurus. Baba Buddha was in charge of the building of the Golden Temple in Amritsar. He was also its first **granthi**. While he supervised the builders, he used to sit under a tree which still exists near the Golden Temple today.*

The tree where Baba Buddha sat still exists.

Guru Har Gobind (1606–44 CE)

Guru Har Gobind was Guru Arjan's son. He was Guru for nearly 40 years, and he realized that Sikhs needed to form an army to defend themselves if necessary. Before he passed away, he chose his grandson to be the next Guru.

Guru Har Rai (1644–61 CE)

Guru Har Rai worked to make Sikhism stronger. While he was Guru, Sikhism spread through northern India. He chose his son to be the next Guru.

Guru Har Krishan (1661–64 CE)

Guru Har Krishan was only five years old when he became Guru, and he passed away when he was only eight.

Guru Tegh Bahadur (1664–75 CE)

Guru Tegh Bahadur was the son of Guru Har Gobind. He was beheaded by the Emperor Aurangzeb in India in 1675 CE, because he refused to change his religion.

▲ This **gurdwara** in Delhi, India, remembers the life of Guru Har Krishan.

Guru Gobind Singh (1675–1708 CE)

Guru Gobind Singh became the tenth Guru when he was only nine years old. He began the **Khalsa**, the group of Sikhs who are committed members of the religion. Guru Gobind Singh chose the holy book, the Guru Granth Sahib, to be Guru after him. He said that in future the Guru Granth Sahib would be the Sikhs' only teacher.

The Khalsa

In 1699 CE, **Guru** Gobind Singh began the **Khalsa**, the group of Sikhs who are committed members of the religion. Crowds of Sikhs were together for the spring festival called Baisakhi. The Guru told them that they needed to be strong to fight people who were trying to get rid of Sikhism.

The Guru drew his sword and asked if any Sikh was willing to die for what they believed. No one answered. The Guru asked again. Still no one answered. The Guru asked a third time, and one man stepped forward. The Guru took him into his tent. There was a thud. The Guru came back with blood on his sword! He asked the question again. Another man came forward. The same thing happened. Three more men were taken away, one by one. The people were terrified. They thought that the Guru had killed all the men.

The Panj Piare

After the fifth time, the Guru went into his tent. Soon afterwards, he returned with all five men! They were dressed in yellow robes, like his own. The Guru said that the men had been prepared to die for their beliefs, so they should be called the **Panj Piare** – the five beloved ones.

These men are dressed like the Panj Piare – the five beloved ones – who were willing to die for what they believed.

The Guru said that the five men would be the first members of a new group. It would be called the Khalsa, which means 'the pure ones'. Guru Gobind Singh said that Sikhs could only belong to the Khalsa if they were without fear and ready to die for their religion. When the people understood what the Guru wanted, many more men and women came forward to join the Khalsa.

The Guru told them that to show that they all belonged to the same family, they should use the same name. Men took the name Singh (which means lion). Women took the name Kaur (which means princess). The Guru said that to show they were all equal, they should drink **amrit** from the same bowl. They should also wear five **symbols** of their faith. Sikhs still wear these five symbols, which are called the five Ks.

▲ *Drinking amrit is still part of Sikh worship today.*

Drinking amrit
*The Guru told members of the Khalsa to drink amrit from the same bowl. Amrit is a special mixture of sugar and water, stirred with a **khanda**. Drinking amrit from the same bowl was important because, in those days, people from different backgrounds never ate or drank together. To do so showed that people were all equal.*

The early days of Sikhism

After the death of **Guru** Gobind Singh, Sikhs began to find life very difficult. The **Mughal** Emperors who ruled India at that time were **Muslims**. They did not agree with the way that Sikhs and **Hindus** worshipped. Sikhs were in danger of being killed because of what they believed.

Ranjit Singh

As the Mughal **Empire** lost its power, Sikhs began winning battles. Small Sikh states were formed. The ruler of one of them was a young soldier called Ranjit Singh, who lived from 1780–1839 CE. He took over other Sikh states and became the ruler of a Sikh empire. It included the whole of the Punjab and much of northern India. He ruled well for 40 years. Many Sikhs think that this was one of the best times in Sikh history.

After Ranjit Singh died, his empire collapsed. In 1849 CE, the British took control of the Punjab as they increased the land ruled by the British Empire in India. They did not really understand that Sikhism was a different religion from Hinduism. Sikh leaders had to work hard to keep the religion separate. It was many years before Sikhs were allowed to organize their religion as they wanted.

Ranjit Singh was an important Sikh ruler. An attack of smallpox had left him blind in one eye.

Khalistan

When the new country of Pakistan was formed in 1947 CE, the border with India cut right through the middle of the Punjab. Many Sikhs were very disappointed. They had hoped that they would be given their own country. Many Sikhs felt they had to leave Pakistan, and there were riots. Thousands of people were killed. It was a time of great bitterness and unhappiness, and many Sikhs felt that they had been treated very unfairly.

▲ *This **gurdwara** is in Kenya, Africa, where many Sikhs live.*

In 1984 CE, after years of problems, the Indian army took over the Punjab and attacked the Golden Temple in Amritsar. They said that this was because some Sikh fighters were hiding there. Many Sikhs were killed. The Golden Temple and the Akal Takht, the holiest places of Sikhism, were badly damaged. The attack made Sikhs all over the world very angry. Many Sikhs today would like to have their own country, which they would call Khalistan.

Sikhs in Africa

During the British Empire, many workers, including Sikhs, were taken from India to Africa, to build roads and railways. Some Sikhs went to live in East Africa, and became successful there. Many of them still live there, but others left when new governments in East Africa made life difficult for Sikhs.

The Guru Granth Sahib

The Adi Granth

In 1604 CE, the fifth **Guru**, Guru Arjan, put together a collection of **hymns**. He made them into the first Sikh holy book, called the **Adi Granth**. Adi means first or most important, and Granth means collection. The **Harimandir Sahib**, or Golden Temple, was built especially as a place to keep the Adi Granth. The Adi Granth still exists today, and Sikhism is the only major religion in the world which still has the first copy of its holy book.

Guru Nanak wrote 974 of the hymns in the Adi Granth. Others were written by other Gurus. There were also some hymns written by **Hindu** and **Muslim** holy men. It is unusual for the holy book of one religion to contain writings by members of other religions. The hymns praise God, and say what God is like. They also tell people about the right way to live.

The Guru Granth Sahib

In 1706 CE, Guru Gobind Singh added some more hymns to the Adi Granth. These were written by the ninth Guru, Guru Tegh Bahadur. Guru Gobind Singh said that this made the Adi Granth complete.

*In a **gurdwara**, the Guru Granth Sahib is placed on a special throne called a **takht**.*

This boy is reading from a gutka, which contains hymns and prayers.

Before he passed away, Guru Gobind Singh said that the Adi Granth should be the next Guru, and that Sikhs should not have any other Guru. Because of this, Sikhs changed its name, and it was called the **Guru Granth Sahib**. (Sahib is a title that shows respect.) Since that time, nothing has been added or taken away from it.

For nearly 200 years, copies of the Guru Granth Sahib were written by hand, very carefully. When copies were first printed, in the nineteenth century CE, it was decided that every copy should be exactly the same. So, today, all copies of the Guru Granth Sahib have the same number of pages – 1430. The hymns are always on the same pages. The Guru Granth Sahib has been translated into other languages to help people understand it, but the original – written in **Gurmukhi** – is normally used in worship.

Gutkas

*Most Sikhs have a book called a **gutka** to read at home. It contains important hymns from the Guru Granth Sahib, and the daily prayers. A gutka is treated with great respect. It is wrapped in a cloth when it is not being read.*

What the Guru Granth Sahib says

Sikhs treat the **Guru Granth Sahib** with great respect, because they believe that it contains God's truth. The Guru Granth Sahib is used in all Sikh worship. It takes the most important place in the **gurdwara**. Weddings are held in front of it, and it is used to help in the naming of babies.

During the day, the Guru Granth Sahib is kept on a special 'seat', called a **manji**, resting on a cloth and three cushions. The manji is part of a throne called a **takht**. The person sitting behind the takht holds a **chauri**, which is a fan made of hair or feathers. This is the same sort of fan that used to be waved over the head of princes in India. Sikhs wave it over the Guru Granth Sahib to show its authority.

When it is closed, the Guru Granth Sahib is covered with special cloths called **rumalas**. At night, it is 'put to bed' in a ceremony called Sukhasan. In the morning, it is taken out in a ceremony called Parkash karna. Carrying the Guru Granth Sahib is a great honour. It is always held above the person's head, as a sign of respect.

Carrying the Guru Granth Sahib is a great honour. Notice the people bowing as it is carried past them.

Some words from the Guru Granth Sahib

All of the **hymns** in the Guru Granth Sahib are written in poetry. The poems are arranged in groups of lines called **shabads**. The first shabad in the Guru Granth Sahib is **Guru** Nanak's description of what God is. This shabad is called the Mool Mantar. It sums up what Sikhs believe about God.

The Mool Mantar

There is one and only one God
Whose name is Truth.
God the creator is without fear, without
*   hate, immortal,*
Without form, and is beyond birth and
*   death,*
And is understood through the Guru's
*   grace.*
(Page 1, Guru Granth Sahib)

▲ *The letters in the centre of this painting mean 'There is only one God.'*

This is how Guru Nanak describes how God told him he was to teach people:
*I was a **minstrel**, out of work, when the Lord took me into*
*   His service.*
To sing His Praises day and night,
He gave me His Order, right from the start.
(Page 150, Guru Granth Sahib)

Guru Nanak believed that men and women should be treated as equal. He said:
From woman, man is born;
within woman, man is conceived;
to woman he is engaged and married.
Woman becomes his friend;
Without woman, there would be no one at all.
(Page 473, Guru Granth Sahib)

The five Ks

The five Ks are symbols of the Sikh religion.

Every man and woman who belongs to the **Khalsa** must wear five **symbols** which show that they are Sikhs. Many other Sikhs choose to wear them, too. They are usually called the five Ks because in **Punjabi** their names all begin with the letter K.

Kesh

Kesh means uncut hair. **Guru** Gobind Singh said that hair should be allowed to grow naturally. For men, this includes not shaving.

Kangha

The **kangha** is a small wooden comb. It keeps the hair fixed in place, and is a symbol of cleanliness. Combing their hair reminds Sikhs that their lives should be tidy and organized, too.

Kirpan

The **kirpan** is a short sword. It reminds Sikhs that they must fight against evil. A kirpan should never be used for attack, only for defence. It may be up to one metre long, but most Sikhs today carry a kirpan which is about ten centimetres long. It is usually kept in a wooden case which is fixed to a strap which the person wears over their shoulder.

Why do Sikhs wear turbans?

At the time of Guru Gobind Singh, many people in India wore turbans. They were a sign of power. The Guru wore one as a sign of the power of the Sikhs. His followers copied him, and so wearing turbans became a custom. Gradually, it became a symbol of Sikhism.

Kara

The **kara** is a plain steel bangle worn on the right wrist. It is a complete circle, which reminds Sikhs that there is one God and one truth, without beginning or end. The steel reminds them of the strength they must have when fighting for what is right.

Kachera

Kachera are short trousers, worn as underwear. They were more practical than the long, loose clothes most people in India wore at the time of Guru Gobind Singh. The Guru said they were a symbol that Sikhs were leaving old ideas behind, and following better ones.

Turban

A **turban** is a piece of cloth about five metres long, wound tightly around the head and tucked in to keep it in place. It is not one of the five Ks, but most male Sikhs and some female Sikhs wear one. Other people may wear a turban, too, but they are especially important for Sikhs. It has become a symbol of the Sikh religion, and Sikhs do not wear anything else on their head.

A Sikh boy tying his turban.

The gurdwara

Sikhs meet for worship in the diwan hall.

The Sikh place of worship is called the **gurdwara**. This really means '**Guru's door**'. A gurdwara does not have to be a special building – many of the first gurdwaras were tents. The important thing about the gurdwara is the fact that the **Guru Granth Sahib**, the Sikh holy book, is there. Wherever the Guru Granth Sahib is placed becomes a gurdwara.

A gurdwara always has a place near its entrance where Sikhs can wash their hands and feet. There is always somewhere for people to leave their shoes. No one wears shoes in the **diwan hall**, the room where people meet for worship. There is always a kitchen and a dining room for preparing and eating the **langar**. Larger gurdwaras may also have a library, classrooms, and sometimes offices, too. Sikhs are expected not to smoke or drink alcohol, so these things are not allowed in a gurdwara.

The langar
Sikh services are followed by a meal called the langar. Sikhs expect that everyone who has attended the service will attend the langar. Food is cooked and served by both men and women, and is offered free to everyone. The meal is always simple, vegetarian Indian food.

Outside the gurdwara

Some gurdwaras are specially built and beautifully decorated. Many gurdwaras are in ordinary houses, especially in countries other than India. All gurdwaras have a yellow flag outside, which has the **khanda**, the Sikh **symbol**, on it. This is called the **Nishan Sahib**. It always flies above the level of the building.

The diwan hall

The diwan hall is often decorated with tinsel and small lights. Sometimes there are pictures of Guru Nanak and the other Gurus on the side walls. It usually has a carpet, but no seats. Everyone attending worship sits on the floor. This is a sign that everyone is equal.

The most important part of the diwan hall is the **takht**, which means the throne. This is always at one end. The Guru Granth Sahib is placed on the takht, on a special 'seat' called a **manji**. The takht is the same sort of throne that a human guru would sit on. It shows that the book is treated with the same respect. In front of the takht is a place where people can place offerings of food or money. These may be used in the langar, or to help pay for it.

The outside of a gurdwara. Notice the Nishan Sahib, the Sikh flag which flies outside every gurdwara.

Worship in the gurdwara

Sikhs do not have a particular day of worship. Many **gurdwaras** are open every day, with services in the morning and evening. Any Sikh who is respected by the others and who can read **Gurmukhi** may lead worship. Many gurdwaras employ a **granthi**. A granthi's job is to read from the **Guru Granth Sahib** and to lead the prayers.

Sikh worship takes place in the **diwan hall**, in front of the Guru Granth Sahib. Before they go in, everyone takes off their shoes. They may wash their hands and feet, or have a bath at home before coming to the gurdwara. Anyone who is not wearing a **turban** covers their head. These things are to show respect for the Guru Granth Sahib.

When they go in to the diwan hall, people go to the front and leave food or money in front of the **takht**

Any Sikh who can read Gurmukhi may read the Guru Granth Sahib in the gurdwara.

where the Guru Granth Sahib is placed. They bow or kneel in front of it. As they go to sit down, they never turn their backs on the takht. This would show a lack of respect.

Sikh worship is led by musicians called ragis.

People sit on the floor to show that everyone is equal and that the Guru Granth Sahib is the most important thing in the room. Men and women usually sit on opposite sides of the room because this is the custom in India, where Sikhism first began.

Worship

Services in a gurdwara are usually in **Punjabi**. Services may last up to five hours, but people do not always stay for the whole time. There are readings and singing of **hymns** from the Guru Granth Sahib, and from other books by the **Gurus**. The singing is called **kirtan** and is very important. It is performed by musicians called **ragis**. The people do not usually join in the singing. There may also be a talk.

Sikh services end with a prayer called the **Ardas**. While this is being said, **karah parshad** is prepared. This is a special sweet made of flour, sugar, water and ghee (specially prepared butter). It is given to everyone as a **symbol** that everyone is equal. After the service, everyone shares the **langar**.

The Ardas

The Ardas is the prayer which ends Sikh services. It lasts about fifteen minutes. It reminds everyone to remember God and the ten Gurus, and to pass on the teachings of the Guru Granth Sahib. Then prayers are said for Sikhs and all people.

The Harimandir Sahib, Amritsar

You can find the places mentioned in this book on the map on page 44.

Sikhs believe that every **gurdwara** is equally important, because each one contains the **Guru Granth Sahib**. However, the **Harimandir Sahib** at Amritsar in India is very special. Harimandir Sahib means Temple of God. A lake was built first, between 1577 and 1588 CE. This lake is called the Pool of Nectar. Then work began on the temple itself, which was completed in 1601 CE. Sikhs today travel from all over the world to worship there.

The temple stands in the middle of the Pool of Nectar. It is reached by a walkway which is 60 metres long. The temple is on a platform which is 20 metres square. The temple itself is 12 metres square. It is surrounded by a marble walkway. It has entrances on all four sides, to show that Sikhism is open to everyone. In 1764 CE, the temple was rebuilt in marble. The Sikh ruler Ranjit Singh ordered that the top half should be covered in gold. Since then, it has been known as the Golden Temple.

The walls of the Golden Temple have verses from the Guru Granth Sahib carved on them. Readings and singing of **hymns** from the Guru Granth Sahib begins at sunrise, and goes on until late at night every day.

▼ *The Golden Temple in the holy city of Amritsar.*

The readings are heard all around the area through loudspeakers. Worshippers listen to the readings, and they may say their own prayers as well. Some worshippers bathe in the lake. Everyone is there to concentrate on God. Even with the crowds who visit, the atmosphere is quiet and respectful. Visiting the temple is the sort of experience that people remember all their lives.

To take part in the procession to carry the Guru Granth Sahib is a great honour.

At five o'clock every morning and at ten o'clock every night there is a special procession. The Guru Granth Sahib is carried to and from the worship room in the Golden Temple to the room where it spends the night. This room is in the Akal Takht, which is a building at the other end of the walkway. The Guru Granth Sahib is carried on a special covered 'stretcher', resting on cushions. It is wrapped in silk, and showered with rose petals. To take part in the procession and help to carry the Guru Granth Sahib is a great honour. The short journey may take up to half an hour while hundreds of worshippers take part.

Taking the vak

Taking the **vak** means using the Guru Granth Sahib to show people how to live. The book is opened at any page. The vak is the first line of the first complete hymn on the left-hand page. Each day's vak is written out and pinned up at the entrance to the **gurdwara** so that everyone attending can read the advice.

27

Five special gurdwaras

After the **Harimandir Sahib**, there are five **gurdwaras** in the world that are thought to be most special. They are the Five **Takhts** (thrones).

▲ *The Akal Takht in Amritsar is an important centre for Sikhs.*

Akal Takht

Akal Takht means 'eternal throne'. The Akal Takht is at the other end of the walkway which leads to the Harimandir Sahib in Amritsar. It is the place where the **Guru Granth Sahib** is kept at night, after it has been in the Harimandir Sahib during the day.

Takht Damdama Sahib

This gurdwara is in the south of the Punjab. **Guru** Gobind Singh lived here for nearly a year in 1705 CE. It was where he put together the complete Guru Granth Sahib.

You can find the places mentioned in this book on the map on page 44.

Takht Keshgarh Sahib

This gurdwara is in Anandpur, near the Himalayan mountains. It is built at the place where the head of Guru Tegh Bahadur was **cremated**. Anandpur is also the place where Guru Gobind Singh began the **Khalsa**.

Takht Keshgarh Sahib in Anandpur.

Takht Hazur Sahib

This gurdwara was built over the place where Guru Gobind Singh's body was cremated. It has a museum where some of the Guru's clothes are kept. The museum is also home to a horse which is descended from one which the Guru owned. This horse is used in **gurpurb** processions that are held in the town.

Takht Patna Sahib

This gurdwara is in the town of Patna, in India. It is the place where Guru Gobind Singh was born. Guru Nanak and Guru Tegh Bahadur also visited Patna.

Sikhs and pilgrimage

People from many religions go on **pilgrimages** *to important places in their religion. Guru Nanak told his followers that they should not do this. He said that what they believed was much more important than visiting a particular place:*

If a man goes to bathe at a place of pilgrimage, and he has the mind of a crook and the body of a thief, of course his outside will be washed by the bathing, but his inside will be twice as unclean... *(Adi Granth, 789)*

Celebrations – Baisakhi

The calendar used by Sikhs is called the Nanakshahi calendar. It counts years starting with the birth of **Guru** Nanak in 1469 CE. For example, the year 2005 CE is 536 Nanakshahi. In 1999 CE, Sikhs changed this calendar so that it follows the sun, not the moon. (This is like the Common Era calendar.) This means that festivals now occur on the same Common Era dates every year. New Year is 1 Chet, which is 14 March in the Common Era calendar.

Baisakhi

Baisakhi falls on 14 April in the Common Era calendar. It is celebrated by Sikhs all over the world. The first Baisakhi festival took place in 1567 CE. In 1699 CE, Guru Gobind Singh began the **Khalsa** at Baisakhi. This is why Baisakhi is now often a popular time for holding the **Amrit** Ceremony for people who wish to become members of the Khalsa. In **gurdwaras** all over the world, there are readings from the **Guru Granth Sahib**, and poems which remind people of the first Baisakhi. Like many other Sikh festivals, there are procession which include the Guru Granth Sahib being carried on a float – a lorry or other open vehicle – followed by people singing religious songs.

Handing out special sweets can be part of the celebrations for Baisakhi.

Changing the Nishan Sahib

The **Nishan Sahib** is always changed at Baisakhi. This is the yellow flag which flies outside every gurdwara. On the day of the festival, a service is held outside the gurdwara. It is led by five men who are dressed like the **Panj Piare**, the first members of the Khalsa. The flagpole is taken down, and the chola (the yellow cloth which covers the pole and the flag) is removed. The flagpole and the flag are washed. The chola is always replaced, and a new flag may be used, too. Then the flag is raised above the level of the gurdwara again. Lots of people help. After the flag has been put back, everyone stands for the **Ardas** prayer.

▲ At Baisakhi the covers on the Nishan Sahib are replaced.

Akhand Path

*An **Akhand Path** is when Sikhs read all the way through the Guru Granth Sahib from beginning to end without stopping. This takes about 48 hours. It is part of most Sikh festivals. An Akhand Path is usually arranged so that it ends early in a morning. The reading can be done by any Sikh who can read **Gurmukhi** well. They take turns, reading for no more than two hours at a time. While an Akhand Path is taking place, Sikhs make a special effort to go to the gurdwara. They listen carefully to the words, and they **meditate**.*

Celebrations – gurpurbs

The **Guru Granth Sahib** is carried on a float during gurpurb processions.

A **gurpurb** remembers the birth or death of one of the **Gurus**. Gurpurb means a holy day in honour of the Guru. Celebrations are often held on the weekend following the actual date of the gurpurb, especially in Western countries.

Birthday gurpurbs

Sikhs celebrate Guru Nanak's birthday in November, and Guru Gobind Singh's birthday in December. There are processions through the streets. The people taking part sing **hymns** written by the Gurus. People watching are often offered special sweets, or fruit and soft drinks. This is to remember Guru Nanak's teaching about how important it is to share food together.

The death of Guru Arjan

Guru Arjan was the fifth Guru. He was the first Sikh martyr. A martyr is someone who dies for what they believe. The ruler of the country had ordered that Guru Arjan must give up his Sikh beliefs. Guru Arjan refused, and so the ruler ordered that he should be killed. He was tortured to death. Part of this torture was not being allowed to drink anything. His death took place in summer when it is very hot in India. As a sign of respect for what the Guru suffered, people watching the processions which are held to remember his death are often given soft drinks.

*Processions to remember Guru Tegh Bahadur's death end at this **gurdwara**, built in Delhi, India, at the place where he was killed.*

The death of Guru Tegh Bahadur

Guru Tegh Bahadur lived at a time when the rulers of India were **persecuting** Sikhs and **Hindus**. Leaders of the Hindus came to Guru Tegh Bahadur for advice, because he was a holy man. The Guru told them to tell the emperor that they would accept the emperor's religion if Guru Tegh Bahadur could be persuaded to accept it, too.

When the emperor heard this, the Guru was arrested. The Guru was offered all sorts of rewards if he would change his religion. Then he was made to watch while three of his followers were tortured to death. Even this did not make him change his mind. The rulers ordered that the Guru should be beheaded. Sikhs are very proud of him because if he had given in, Hindus as well as Sikhs would have had to give up what they believed.

Processions

*Gurpurb processions are always organized in the same way. They are led by five people dressed like the **Panj Piare**. They wear yellow robes, usually with a blue belt, and yellow **turbans**. Behind them is a float carrying the **Guru Granth Sahib**. Behind this come the people, singing religious songs.*

Celebrations – melas

Sikhs celebrate two main sorts of festival. **Gurpurbs** celebrate the birth or death of a **Guru**. These are the most important festivals. Other festivals are **melas**, which means fairs. Melas often take place at the same time as **Hindu** festivals, but Sikhs celebrate them in their own way. Many melas take place just in particular areas.

Divali

Divali means festival of lights. It takes place on 7 November. The Sikh celebrations of the festival were started by Guru Amar Das. The first stone of the **Harimandir Sahib**, or Golden Temple, in Amritsar was laid during Divali in 1577 CE. At Divali, Sikhs also remember the story of how Guru Har Gobind, the sixth Guru, was released from prison in 1619 CE. When he returned home the people lit lamps in every house to welcome him. Sikhs today put hundreds of lights around the Golden Temple.

Lights and firework displays at the Golden Temple are part of the celebrations for Divali.

Sports events are held to celebrate Hola Mohalla.

Hola Mohalla

The festival called Hola Mohalla is celebrated in Anandpur in India. It is held on 17 March, and every year it is attended by thousands of people. It was started by Guru Gobind Singh in 1680 CE. He used it as a chance for Sikhs to practise their fighting skills. Today, there are sports events and displays. There are also music and poetry competitions. The festival ends with a large procession, led by people carrying the **Nishan Sahibs** from all the **gurdwaras** in the area.

The Guru and the princes
Guru Har Gobind was in prison. In 1619 the Emperor decided to free him. But the Guru refused to leave unless 52 innocent princes could go, too. The emperor said that the princes who could hold on to the Guru's cloak could leave. But they all had to leave by a gate so narrow that only one man could squeeze through at a time. The Guru had long cords stitched to his cloak so that all the princes could hold it. Everyone was freed.

Special occasions – birth and childhood

The naming ceremony

The naming ceremony for Sikhs takes place when the baby is a few weeks old. Babies normally have a 'pet name' which is used before this. Parents usually take a new **rumala** (the cloth used for covering the **Guru Granth Sahib** when it is not being read) to the **gurdwara**.

When a baby is being named, the **Ardas** prayer at the end of the service includes the names of the parents, and thanks God for the gift of the baby. The parents go forward to the front of the gurdwara, and lay the baby on the floor in front of the Guru Granth Sahib.

The **granthi** opens the Guru Granth Sahib at any page. He or she reads the first new verse on the left-hand page, and then tells the parents which was the first letter of the first word. The parents choose a name for the baby which begins with this letter. When the parents have chosen the name, the granthi announces it to the worshippers and says, "Jo bole so nihal" (this shows that everyone agrees, but it cannot really be translated into English). The worshippers shout, "Sat siri akal" (which means 'God is truth'). Everyone shares **karah parshad** and congratulates the new parents.

Babies are sometimes given a drop of amrit at the naming ceremony.

The Amrit Ceremony

This is the ceremony in which people become members of the **Khalsa**. Those taking **amrit** must be old enough to understand the importance of the ceremony, so they are at least in their teens. Many Sikhs do not take amrit until they are much older, and some never take amrit at all.

Apart from those who wish to join, only Sikhs who are members of the Khalsa themselves are present at the Amrit ceremony. Five Sikhs represent the **Panj Piare**. A sixth Sikh reads from the Guru Granth Sahib. One of the Panj Piare repeats the duties

▲ *Sikhs become members of the Khalsa at the Amrit Ceremony.*

which members of the Khalsa must keep. Then those who are joining the Khalsa kneel on their right knee, with the left knee raised. This shows that they are ready to rise to defend their beliefs. Each person drinks some amrit, and it is sprinkled onto their eyes, hair and hands. After more prayers, the ceremony ends with everyone eating karah parshad. After they have taken amrit, Sikhs are expected to keep all the duties of their religion.

Sikh names

Sikhs use the same names for both men and women. However, men also have the name Singh, and women also have the name Kaur. Many Sikhs use these names as their surname. Others prefer to use their family name as a surname.

Special occasions – marriage

Many Sikh weddings are agreed between families. The bride must be at least eighteen years old, and both the bride and the bridegroom must agree to the marriage.

Sikh weddings must always take place in front of the **Guru Granth Sahib**. In India, they are often held in the open air. In other countries, they are usually held in the **gurdwara**. Any Sikh may perform the marriage.

The bridegroom usually wears a red **turban**. He wears a scarf around his neck. He sits in front of the Guru Granth Sahib. The bride enters, with her sister or another female relation. She wears red, often with beautiful gold jewellery. They bow to the Guru Granth Sahib, and then she sits next to the bridegroom.

There are prayers and readings, and the leader gives a talk about marriage. The couple show that they agree to the marriage by bowing in front of the Guru Granth Sahib. The bride's father puts one end of the bridegroom's scarf in his hand and gives the other end to the bride. They hold on to it for the rest of the ceremony.

Helping a bridegroom to get ready for his wedding is an important job.

The Lavan

The most important part of the wedding is reading the **Lavan**. This is a wedding **hymn** written by **Guru** Ram Das. It has four verses. Each one explains something about marriage. They are read one at a time, then sung. During the singing, the bride and the bridegroom walk around the Guru Granth Sahib. When they have done this for the fourth time, they are married. Everyone joins in the **Ardas** prayer and shares **karah parshad**. A meal follows, which may be held in the **langar** room.

▲ *The bride and bridegroom hold on to the bridegroom's scarf to show they are being joined in marriage.*

Divorce

Divorce is ending a marriage when both the husband and the wife are still alive. Sikhs do not approve of divorce, and it is rare among Sikh families. If the marriage cannot be saved, divorce is allowed, and either person may marry again in the gurdwara.

Sikh brides

Preparing a bride for her wedding is very important. On the evening before the wedding, the bride's friends and female relations have a party at her house. She is given money and special sweet foods, and they paint beautiful patterns on her hands and feet. These patterns last for several days.

Special occasions – death

What Sikhs believe about death

Sikhs believe that a person's **soul** moves on to another body after death. This is called **reincarnation**. **Guru** Nanak said that reincarnation explains why life often seems unfair. Things someone did in a past life can follow them to affect their present life. Sikhs believe that by living a good life and helping others a person can become closer to God. With God's help they can become good enough to break out of the cycle of being reborn. Then they will be able to live with God forever.

Sikhs say that death is like going to sleep. When you are tired, you go to sleep, and wake up ready for another day. Sikhs say that in the same way at the end of life a person dies and is reborn. Sikhism teaches that people who are left may feel sad, but they should also remember that the person who has died has gone on to another life.

Sikh funerals

After a person has died, their body is washed and dressed in the five Ks, the **symbols** of Sikhism. Then it is wrapped in a white sheet. Sikhs are usually **cremated**. In India, cremation usually takes place on the day of death. The body is taken to a **funeral pyre** on the bank of a river or, in cities, it is taken to a crematorium.

A Sikh funeral. The flowers spell Baba which is a title often used for Sikh grandfathers.

Male relatives help to carry the coffin.

In Western countries, the funeral takes place as soon as possible after death, and the body is taken to a crematorium. Male relatives usually help to carry the coffin, just as in India they would help to lift the body on to the funeral pyre.

The **Ardas** and the Kirtan Sohila prayers are repeated. After the body has been cremated, the ashes which are left, and the **kirpan** and **kara** (which will not burn because they are made of metal), are usually scattered on a river or the sea. Sikhs living in other countries sometimes have the ashes flown back to the Punjab so that they can be scattered there.

Sikhs do not normally put up headstones or other memorials to people who have died. They believe people should be remembered for the good things they did during their life.

The Kirtan Sohila
The Kirtan Sohila is the Sikh night-time prayer. It is read at funerals to remind Sikhs that death is like sleep.

Ways to be a Sikh

Sikhs try to follow the teachings of the **Gurus** and the **Guru Granth Sahib** in their everyday life. In 1945 CE, Sikh leaders put together the Rahit Maryada. It sets out basic rules for how Sikhs should live.

Members of the **Khalsa** should repeat five special prayers every day. They should treat every person in the same way, and should not take any notice of what their background is. (In India, many people still think that a person's background decides a lot about the sort of person they are.) There are also four actions which are forbidden for members of the Khalsa. They must not cut their hair, they must not use drugs other than medicines, they must be faithful to the person they are married to, and they must not eat meat where the animal has been killed by cutting its throat. Many Sikhs who are not members of the Khalsa choose to follow these rules, too.

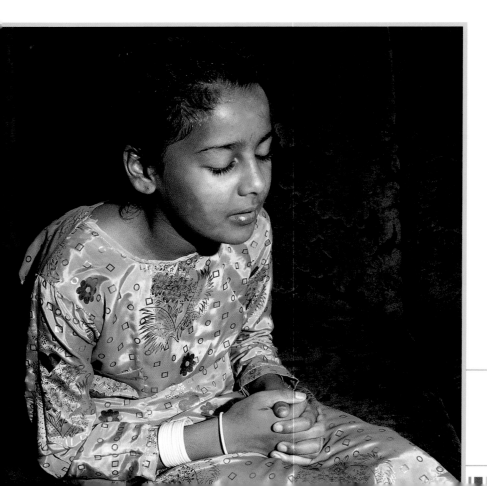

Sikhs are expected to look after their body, because it is where the **soul** is. Healthy eating, doing good things and thinking good thoughts are part of looking after the body. **Meditation** is important, especially meditating on the name of God.

Meditation is an important part of Sikh worship.

Sewa

Sewa means doing things for other people. It is a basic part of Sikh teaching. Sewa means that Sikhs should try to do what they can for other people. This could mean giving money, but it may be more important to give their time. Sewa often involves doing jobs which people do not like doing. It may also involve things such as cooking and serving the **langar** at the **gurdwara**, or looking after people who are poor or ill.

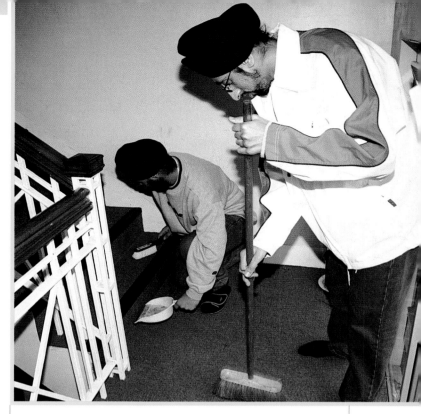

All Sikhs should do things to help others. Jobs such as cooking and cleaning can be part of this.

Sewa often involves talking to people about God. Sikhs do not try to persuade other people to become Sikhs. Sikhism teaches that each person should follow the religion that is right for them. Guru Nanak did not try to persuade people to change their religion. He taught that what is important is the way people live. This matters far more than what religion someone belongs to.

The Anand

*This **hymn** is used by Sikhs every day when they meditate.*

O my mind, concentrate
    on God, stick to God!
Your sufferings will vanish.
If God accepts you, you
    will succeed.
God is almighty and can
    do anything for you, so
    why forget God?
O my mind, keep fixed
    on God always.
(Adi Granth 917)

Map

The globe on the right shows the location of the map below. The map shows some places that are important in the history of Sikhism.

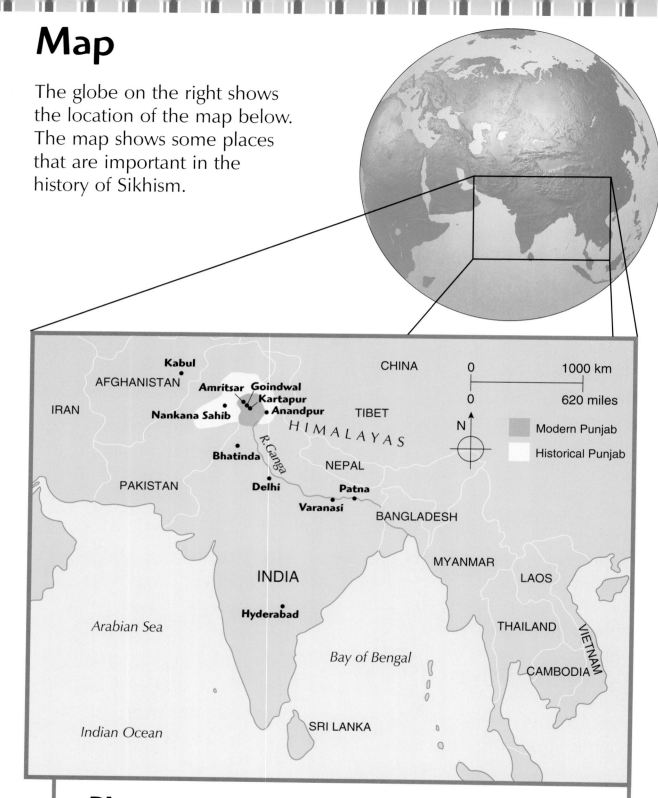

Place names

Some places on this map, or mentioned in the book, have been known by different names:

Nankana Sahib – Talwindi   Varanasi – Benares

Timechart

Major events in World history

BCE	3000–1700	Indus valley civilization (Hinduism)
	c2685–1196	Egyptian civilization
	c2000	Abraham lived (Judaism)
	1800	Stonehenge completed
	c528	Siddhattha Buddha born (Buddhism)
	c450–146	Greek Empire
	200	Great Wall of China begun
	c300–300CE	Roman Empire
	c4	Jesus of Nazareth born (Christianity)
CE	570	Muhammad born (Islam)
	1066	Battle of Hastings and the Norman conquest of England
	1325–1521	Aztec Empire
	1400	Black Death kills one person in three in China, North Africa and Europe
	1469	Guru Nanak born (Sikhism)
	1564	William Shakespeare born
	1914–18	World War I
	1939–45	World War II
	1946	First computer invented
	1969	First moon landings
	2000	Millennium celebrations all over the world

Major events in Sikhism

CE	1469	Guru Nanak born
	1499	Guru Nanak's vision
	1539	Guru Nanak passes away
	1575	Beginning of the building of Amritsar
	1604	Adi Granth put together and placed in the Harimandir Sahib
	1699	Guru Gobind Singh establishes the Khalsa
	1706	Guru Granth Sahib completed
	1780–1839	Life of Ranjit Singh (great Sikh ruler)
	1852	First printed copies of Guru Granth Sahib made
	1909	Sikhs allowed to control their own religion for the first time
	1925	Sikhs allowed to look after gurdwaras for the first time
	1945	Rahit Maryada put together by Sikh ruling council in Punjab
	1947	The making of Pakistan splits the Punjab in two
	1984	The Golden Temple is attacked by the Indian army

Glossary

Adi Granth	Sikh holy book
Akhand Path	non-stop reading of the Guru Granth Sahib
amrit	special mixture of sugar crystals and water
Ardas	prayer offered during most Sikh worship
caste	traditional group in Indian society
chauri	fan waved over the Guru Granth Sahib as a sign of respect
cremation	burn a body after death
diwan hall	worship room in a gurdwara
empire	group of countries under one ruler, called the emperor
eternal	lasting for ever
funeral pyre	special fire built to cremate dead bodies
granthi	person who reads and looks after the Guru Granth Sahib
gurdwara	Sikh place of worship
Gurmukhi	written form of Punjabi
gurpurb	festival celebrating the birth or death of a Guru
Guru	respected teacher (for Sikhs, one of ten special teachers)
Guru Granth Sahib	holy book of the Sikhs
gutka	collection of Sikh hymns and prayers
Harimandir Sahib	'temple of God' – holiest temple of the Sikhs
Hindu	follower of the religion of Hinduism
hymns	religious poems
kachera	shorts worn as underwear (one of the five Ks)
kangha	wooden comb (one of the five Ks)
kara	steel bangle (one of the five Ks)
karah parshad	'holy sweet' – special food shared at the end of Sikh worship
kesh	uncut hair (one of the five Ks)

Khalsa	'Sikh fellowship' – full members of the religion
khanda	the Sikh symbol (also the name for the two-edged sword which is part of the symbol)
kirpan	short sword (one of the five Ks)
kirtan	singing during Sikh worship
langar	meal served as part of Sikh worship
Lavan	wedding hymn written by Guru Ram Das
manji	special 'seat' on which Guru Granth Sahib rests
minstrel	travelling musician
meditation	training the mind to concentrate in a special way
mela	'fair' – Sikh festival
Mughal	Muslim rulers of India during the seventeenth and eighteenth centuries CE
Muslim	follower of the religion of Islam
Nishan Sahib	Sikh flag
Panj Piare	'five beloved ones' – the first members of the Khalsa
persecute	punish someone for what they believe
pilgrimage	journey made for religious reasons
Punjabi	Indian language spoken by most Sikhs
ragi	musician who leads the singing during worship
reincarnation	belief that a soul is reborn in another body
rumala	cloth used for covering the Guru Granth Sahib
sewa	service – caring for others
shabad	hymn from the Guru Granth Sahib
soul	person's spirit which lives on after death
spirit	a being without a body
symbol	something which stands for something else
takht	'throne' where the Guru Granth Sahib is placed
turban	length of material wound around the head to cover it
vak	teaching from the Gurus obtained by opening the Guru Granth Sahib at any page
vision	dream-like religious experience

Index

Titles in the *Religions of the World* series include:

Hardback   0 431 14953 4

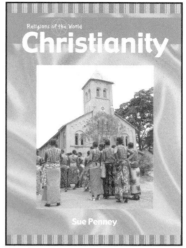

Hardback   0 431 14950 X

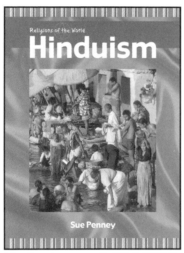

Hardback   0 431 14955 0

Hardback   0 431 14952 6

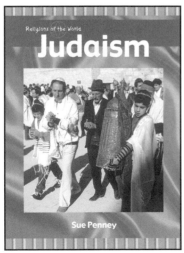

Hardback   0 431 14954 2

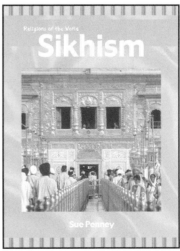

Hardback   0 431 14951 8

Find out about the other titles in this series on our website www.heinemann.co.uk/library